THE VALUE OF ME

NIKEISHA NICKELS

Address all personal correspondence to:
Nikeisha Nickels
www.LifeInOverflow.com

Individuals and church groups may order books from Nikeisha Nickels directly, or from the publisher. Retailers and wholesalers should order from our distributors. Refer to the Deeper Revelation Books website for distribution information, as well as an online catalog of all our books.

Published by:
Deeper Revelation Books
Revealing "the deep things of God" (1 Cor. 2:10)
P.O. Box 4260
Cleveland, TN 37320 423-478-2843
Website: www.deeperrevelationbooks.org
Email: info@deeperrevelationbooks.org

Deeper Revelation Books assists Christian authors in publishing and distributing their books. Final responsibility for design, content, permissions, editorial accuracy, and doctrinal views, either expressed or implied, belongs to the author.

Acknowledgements

To my God, my King, who has given me value and enriched me with an everlasting life and an everlasting love. May I continue to give You all of the glory and honor all the days of my life.

To my dear parents, who have shown me my value through their love for me.

To my sister, who has never let me forget my value.

To my family, who has supported me through prayers and guidance.

To my faith family and friends, who sharpen, challenge, and inspire me.

Thank you.

Table of Contents

Introduction

God is not concerned about your status, outward appearance, skill, or ability. God is concerned about your heart. Our value is not in our ability but our identity as a child of God. Who are we in God's eyes? We are created with a purpose, we are chosen, we are fearless, we are protected, we are confident. Do you trust that God sees you this way? Does God know you trust Him? Trust is confidence, assurance, and reliance, all found in God. The more we practice trusting God, the more we see His reflection in us, and, therefore, the more we understand our own value. God makes us valuable.

Use this resource to encourage and strengthen you. You could be a parent who needs to know that you are appreciated and purposed for the role of a parent. As a single person, your marital status does not dictate your effectiveness in the kingdom of God. If you are a teenager, don't let society tell you who are and how you should define yourself. Families will have victory by knowing God's view of value and will become more effective in loving one another.

Commit your heart to discovering the value that is in you and allow God to lead and guide you in your purpose for His will. Study along with your Bible. Mark verses that speak to you. If you can, write next to those verses what you received from them. My prayer is that the Holy Spirit will open the scriptures so you can see how it is a witness to our great God, His ability, and His willingness to be all that we need so that we can be complete in life.

In this resource, you will cover five sections:

What is Value? You will understand the term "value" and why there is a struggle with identity.

I am a Child of God. Here we explore who God is, and, therefore, who you are.

The Great Exchange of Jesus' Life for My Life. This is a discussion on the impact of being a child of God and the blessing that comes with it.

Practice Trusting God. Discover what confidence in God looks like and create a pattern for building your trust and confidence in God.

What is My Value? You will understand how your value can impact people around you and the generations to come.

Let's start. Write down your response to the questions below:

What is the definition of value?

What comes to mind when you think of value?

What is your value?

What Is Value?

While on a plane with plenty of time to think, I asked God, "Why do we struggle with identity?" God reminded me of a movie. The movie was about a young girl who discovers that she is the rightful heir to the throne. She is the heir because of her father. She has known of her father her whole life, but she did not know the power of his name. She never knew the value of her relationship to him, and, therefore, she did not know her own value. It was not until she really knew his value and his importance that she knew for herself how she was needed and treasured.

Just as the young girl did not understand her true value, we do not always understand our God-given value. Many do not know these three things:

1. God's value

2. The significance of our relationship with Him

3. Our own value

The more we discover who God is, the more we know the value of our relationship with Him, and, therefore, our own value. This is the abundant life. John 10:10 states, "The thief does not come except to steal, and to kill, and to destroy. I have come that they may have life, and that they may have it more abundantly." It is not for us just to live but to live a life full of value and purpose. Ephesians 2:10 notes, "For we are His workmanship [His own master work, a work of art], created in Christ Jesus [reborn from above—spiritually transformed, renewed, ready to be used] for good works, which God prepared [for us] beforehand [taking paths which He set], so that we would walk in them [living the good life which He prearranged and made ready for us]" (Amp).

This is a destined life. We are chosen, valued, protected, fought for, bought with the highest price; we are fearless, forgiven, wonderfully made, secured, accepted, significant, and loved. All of this because we are chosen. Chosen by God. God gave His only Son because He saw us as the most precious jewels. He exchanged the life of His Son for us because He loved us so much that He wanted us for Himself. It was as if He walked into a jewelry store and said, "This is the one I want, and I will pay the price." That purchase makes us valuable. He wants all the best for us, and He wants us to know how valuable we are to Him. It's not about what we have done or any decision we have made (right or wrong) but simply because of His love for us. This love He gives us is pure love.

Defining Value

Using King David from the Bible as our common reference point, we will see how God saw David. The Bible gives us real life lessons that we can learn from to improve our lives. One way to learn how to treasure our value is by seeing an example of what not to do. In this section, we will understand how King Saul was chosen but did not live out his full purpose. Then we will discuss how David's life was prepared for him.

First, let's define value. Our value is not defined by how we see ourselves but by our identity as a child of God. The struggle with knowing and accepting our own value is because we struggle with accepting God's value or the significance of our relationship with Him. God is the Great Creator and the Designer of Life. Our relationship with the One who created the paths for our lives makes us greater than we can possibly imagine. This relationship is the understructure to accepting our identity as a child of God, and, therefore, who we are in God.

What is "value"?

_____

_____

_____

_____

_____

What must we do to align God's will to our lives?

_____

_____

_____

_____

Take away this: God valued us so much that He gave His only Son for us. How amazing is God to give His most precious as an exchange for our lives! Not for anything we did or could do, but simply because He loves us.

The Foundation to Accepting My Identity

The suggested reading is 1 Samuel 8-15.

Saul was equipped to be king because God was with him. Along his journey in his position, he allowed pride to get the best of him. This is evident because Saul did not offer sacrifices properly (1 Samuel 10:8, 1 Samuel 13:6-10). Listed below is the evidence of Saul's abuse of his position as king.

1. Saul violated a command. He allowed self-importance and pride to supersede God's will. (1 Samuel 13:8-14)

2. Saul ordained an oath in an effort to win the favor of the Lord (1 Samuel 14:24-30). This poor judgment led to troops not following the Lord's command (1 Samuel 14:31-35).

3. Saul sentenced his son to death (1 Samuel 14:43-45). This was a foolish act.

4. Saul did not destroy the Amalekites as requested (1 Samuel 15:1-9; notice verses 3 and 15). He was disobedient.

5. Saul does not own his fall (1 Samuel 15:20-31; notice verses 20-21). He did not immediately repent.

Saul's actions proved he was not ready to be king (1 Samuel 15:10-11). Again, the relationship we have with God is the understructure to accepting our identity as a child of God and, therefore, who we are in God.

We should not have idols in place of God. Don't allow position or status to determine who you are. Don't allow money or your home or your neighborhood or the people around you prove to you that you are valuable. You must constantly remind yourself that God is the center of everything you do. If not, an idol can lead to unhealthy opinions or self-glory. Let us look at pride. Proverbs 16:18 states, "Pride goes before destruction, and a haughty spirit before a fall." First Peter 5:5 informs us, "God resists the proud, but gives grace to the humble." So then, what follows pride?

- Jealousy
- Lust for praise
- Seeking attention
- Defensiveness
- Unnatural competition
- Inability to honor others
- Revenge

You must understand who really comes first. There will be opportunities to glorify yourself, but the glory belongs to God first.

Did Saul seek God with all of his heart?
Reference 1 Samuel 15:10-11.

How can people pleasing get us off track?
Reference 1 Samuel 15:24.

What would have made King Saul more effective in his role?

Take away this: Be confident and unwavering in where God has called you.

Preparing for God's Will for My Life

The suggested reading is 1 Samuel 16.

Before David's name was mentioned to Samuel (the one who anointed David as king), God determined his purpose (1 Samuel 16:1). David would not have been Samuel's first choice. David stature was nothing compared to Saul's (1 Samuel 9:2). David was not yet mature. He was ruddy in feature (1 Samuel 16:12). God knew David had a heart after His own heart. Before David knew his own true purpose, God placed a purpose on David's life and created a specific path so that he could be successful. Again, let us look at Ephesians 2:10 which states "For we are His workmanship, created in Christ Jesus for good works, which God prepared beforehand that we should walk in them." God has a path for all of us. You can choose to live the life that God has prepared for you.

Before David became king of Israel, he prepared and trained for that position of king. In between David's anointment of king and appointment to king, he learned how to lead, strategize, build relationships, communicate, develop others, and create vision. Before becoming king, David trained and prepared for God's will for his life. If you find yourself not at your appointment, ask God what He is giving you as an opportunity. Focus on training and preparing in your season of opportunity for God's purpose in your life.

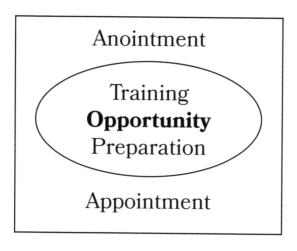

The diagram depicts where opportunity exists.

What must we do to align God's will to our lives?

What is the purpose of having a life in God?

Take away this: Prepare your heart and be available to be used. Be humble. Respect God's Word. Believe in Him and trust His promises. Live a good life so that you are expanding God's kingdom.

Living in God's Will for My Life

The suggested reading is 1 Samuel 16.

David did what was requested of him. He was the only one in the field at his home, so he must have been trusted to complete the task. He mastered his harp skill, which must have taken a lot of practice. His skills led to him having favor with Saul (1 Samuel 16:22). This favor led to valuable training and connections.

David's training was essential to ensuring that he was well equipped to be king. He would set a new standard for kingship. Although David was a good shepherd, he was not called to lead sheep. It was practice. This was preparation for leading God's people. Although David was skilled to be a harpist, this was a stepping stone in his life's journey. Using David's musical talent, the Lord allowed such a perfect intersection for David and Saul.

Be careful of what others try to make your position (examples: "You will never be anything," or "You're the youngest so you are not fit for the position"). God looks at how prepared your heart is for the position (1 Samuel 16:7). Pray against what does not align with God's will for you. In difficult moments, we can allow others to tell us what our value is during seasons of training. God knows we are not a finished work, which is why He is constantly guiding us. Do not allow others to tell you what you are not able to do based on your ability now. Of course, we are not able to be all that God wants us to be without Him. We trust that God is preparing us for His perfect will.

How do you know what is God's will for you?

What opportunities are you in right now that can give God the glory?

What traits/skills/talents are you mastering? How can those be used for God?

Take away this: Studying the Word helps us stay in prayer. The more we pray, the more we want to study God's Word. We become closer to God's heart and His will for us. Honor God with everything you have, which includes your gifts, talents, knowledge, and understanding.

JOURNAL

Take time to meditate on John 10:10 and Ephesians 2:10. Read them in different Bible versions. Write how the verses resonate with you.

I Am a Child of God

In Section One, we defined value from God's perspective. We also discussed how God prepares us for the path He creates for us through opportunities. We come into agreement with God by embracing the opportunities God gives us and putting Him first always in those opportunities. In this section, we will explore who God is so we are 100 percent confident in who we are.

Saul was chosen but did not live out his full purpose. We mentioned pride was one of Saul's issues. It led to jealousy, lust for praise, seeking attention, defensiveness, unnatural competition, the inability to honor others, and revenge. We answered a few questions together to understand in real life how we know God's will for us. Our self-practice was centered on understanding John 10:10 (our abundant life) and Ephesians 2:10 (our purposed life).

We live our full purpose by knowing who we are. There are many DNA tests designed to help us discover who we are. They are able to confirm relationships and to help us discover where we came from, our ancestry. Let us look at this spiritually. Who are we? We are children of God because Jesus shed His blood for us. His blood redeemed us to God and to the family of God. Your value is not determined by the people you came from or your family, but because you a part of the family of God.

Respond out loud after reading each question.

Who am I according to Ephesians 1:3-6?
I am highly *blessed.*

Who am I according to Jeremiah 29:11?
I am a person of *purpose.*

Who am I according to Psalm 139:14?
I am *fearfully and wonderfully made.*

Who am I according to 2 Corinthians 5:17?
I am a *new creation* in Christ.

Who am I according to Philippians 4:13?
I am *empowered.*

The possibilities of how you can be blessed are endless. You don't need a genealogy test to tell you what you already know. You are a child of the Most High, a child of the King of Kings and Lord of Lords, a child of the One who created the heavens and earth, a child of the Mighty One, a child of the Everlasting, a child of the Wonder Maker, a child of the Deliverer, a child of the Healer, a child of the Savior, a child of the All-Knowing. Who are you? You are a child of God. Let us explore who God is so we know who we are. Also, based on who He is, we will speak forth our faith.

God Is, I Am

The possibilities of who we can be in God are endless. Once we understand who God really is, we can then know who we are. Read Ephesians 1:3-6, Jeremiah 29:11, Psalm 139:14, 2 Corinthians 5:17, and Philippians 4:13. These verses tell us who we are.

How is our victory guaranteed?

_____

_____

_____

_____

_____

_____

Knowing who God is helps us to better understand who we are created to be.

Write a letter to God telling Him who He is to you.

_____

_____

_____

_____

_____

_____

_____

_____

_____

Take away this: Be confident that you belong to God and He wants the best for you.

Fearless in Faith

The suggested reading is 1 Samuel 17.

But David said to Saul, "Your servant used to keep his father's sheep, and when a lion or a bear came and took a lamb out of the flock, I went out after it and struck it, and delivered the lamb from its mouth; and when it arose against me, I caught it by its beard, and struck and killed it. Your servant has killed both lion and bear; and this uncircumcised Philistine will be like one of them, seeing he has defied the armies of the living God." Moreover, David said, "The Lord, who delivered me from the paw of the lion and from the paw of the bear, He will deliver me from the hand of this Philistine." And Saul said to David, "Go, and the Lord be with you!" (1 Samuel 17:34-37).

"Then David said to the Philistine, 'You come to me with a sword, with a spear, and with a javelin. But I come to you in the name of the Lord of hosts, the God of the armies of Israel, whom you have defied.'" (1 Samuel 17:45).

In 1 Samuel 17, David, although considered an ordinary person, has a solution to the problem of how to defeat the Philistine. David saw Goliath as powerless with no covenant with God. David saw himself as God saw him, a mighty warrior. God was so dominate in David's life at this time that he was able to easily defeat a giant. David was fearless. Goliath was no threat to David. In our life, we have an option to "show" God. The bigger the problem, the greater the opportunity to show who God is in your life, resulting in a greater testimony.

The next time you are questioning who you are and why you exist, remind yourself that you are a chosen vessel for the Lord. Our God has a mighty task that you have been equipped to solve. Stop looking at what you don't have and look at what you do have. You have God on your side. The negative thoughts are powerless against the thoughts of God for you. Approach the negative thoughts in the name of the Lord of hosts, as David approached his own enemy. The name of the Lord will deliver you and save you from negative thinking and defeat.

What impossible situation has God shown you where He is at work?

What qualifications has God shown you that He can accomplish that impossible task?

How does faith in God grow? (Hint: Our faith grows through practicing what we believe.)

_____

_____

_____

_____

_____

_____

_____

_____

Take away this: Faith gives us courage. Our faith grows through practicing what we believe. We practice our faith. We rely on and believe in God. We choose to follow the route God has for us by being in agreement with God's will and living into what God says we are. We stay convinced that God values us.

My Value in God

The suggested reading is 1 Samuel 19-22.

First Samuel 22 indicates that David stayed in the Cave of Adullam until God informed him of his next step. David needed God during this time. While sheltered in this cave, he wrote several Psalms (including Psalm 18 on thanksgiving, Psalm 52 on trust, Psalm 54 on crying out to God, and Psalms 57 and 59 on prayer). While in the cave, David was not yet appointed king, yet the people saw him as a leader (reference 1 Samuel 22:2). In this place, the people had one another. They learned how to depend on David, and David learned how to lead people. God is continuing to show David his value.

In the cave, David grew more into his purpose. As we grow into our purpose, we increase in the skills needed to complete the purpose. The hard times in life are preparation for something greater. It could be that we need to learn how to be steadfast in our faith, unwavering in difficulties, trusting God to be faithful, or dependent only on Him to solve the problem. Don't allow the situation to alter your relationship with God. God is still the same. You are still His. God still wants you to have all of the blessings that He promised. Lean on God when you feel you are having a hard time in life. Prove to God that He is all you need to be satisfied in life whether life is pleasant or bitter.

Does God know you need Him?

_____

_____

_____

_____

_____

_____

_____

Does God know why you need Him?

_____

_____

_____

_____

_____

_____

_____

_____

Take away this: Really depend on God to show you who you are and seek Him for your value.

Psalm 18: Know God

In the following pages, you will confess who God is and who you are according to Scripture. As you read Psalm 18, describe who God is in each section and what that makes you. This gives an example of how you can depend on God to be what Scripture states He will be.

Once you know who God is, then you will know who you are. Give an example to make it relevant. Example: if God is a Way Maker, then you are not bound, and you can live beyond the negatives of what the world says about you. Another example is if God is a Deliverer, then you are delivered, and sickness cannot stay in you. To get you going, here is one more example: if God is a Protector, then you are protected, and any attack of the enemy will not prosper.

After completing this exercise, take a moment to ponder on which part resonates with you the most and why.

Psalm 18:1-2

"I will love You, O Lord, my strength.

The Lord is my rock and my fortress and my deliverer;

My God, my strength, in whom I will trust;

My shield and the horn of my salvation, my stronghold."

Who is God?

God is a _____.

Who am I?

I am _____.

Example:

_____

_____

_____

_____

_____

_____

Psalm 18:3-5

"I will call upon the LORD, who is worthy to be praised;

So shall I be saved from my enemies.

The pangs of death surrounded me,

And the floods of ungodliness made me afraid.

The sorrows of Sheol surrounded me;

The snares of death confronted me."

Who is God?

God is a _____ .

Who am I?

I am _____ .

Example:

_____

_____

_____

_____

_____

_____

_____

Psalm 18:6-15

"In my distress I called upon the LORD,

And cried out to my God;

He heard my voice from His temple,

And my cry came before Him, even to His ears.

Then the earth shook and trembled;

The foundations of the hills also quaked and were shaken,

Because He was angry.

Smoke went up from His nostrils,

And devouring fire from His mouth;

Coals were kindled by it.

He bowed the heavens also, and came down

With darkness under His feet.

And He rode upon a cherub, and flew;

He flew upon the wings of the wind.

He made darkness His secret place;

His canopy around Him was dark waters

And thick clouds of the skies.

From the brightness before Him,

His thick clouds passed with hailstones and coals of fire."

"The LORD thundered from heaven,

And the Most High uttered His voice,

Hailstones and coals of fire.

He sent out His arrows and scattered the foe,

Lightnings in abundance, and He vanquished them.

Then the channels of the sea were seen,

The foundations of the world were uncovered

At Your rebuke, O LORD,

At the blast of the breath of Your nostrils."

Who is God?

God is a _____ .

Who am I?

I am _____ .

Example:

_____

_____

_____

_____

_____

Psalm 18:16-24

"He sent from above, He took me;

He drew me out of many waters.

He delivered me from my strong enemy,

From those who hated me,

For they were too strong for me.

They confronted me in the day of my calamity,

But the LORD was my support.

He also brought me out into a broad place;

He delivered me because He delighted in me.

The LORD rewarded me according to my righteousness;

According to the cleanness of my hands

He has recompensed me.

For I have kept the ways of the LORD,

And have not wickedly departed from my God.

For all His judgments were before me,

And I did not put away His statutes from me.

I was also blameless before Him,

And I kept myself from my iniquity.

Therefore the LORD has recompensed me according to my righteousness,

According to the cleanness of my hands in His sight."

Who is God?

God is a _____ .

Who am I?

I am _____ .

Example:

_____

_____

_____

_____

_____

_____

Psalm 18:25-30

"With the merciful You will show Yourself merciful;

With a blameless man You will show Yourself blameless;

With the pure You will show Yourself pure;

And with the devious You will show Yourself shrewd.

For You will save the humble people,

But will bring down haughty looks.

For You will light my lamp;

The LORD my God will enlighten my darkness.

For by You I can run against a troop,

By my God I can leap over a wall.

As for God, His way is perfect;

The word of the LORD is proven;

He is a shield to all who trust in Him."

Who is God?

God is a _____ .

Who am I?

I am _____ .

Example:

_____

_____

_____

_____

_____

_____

_____

Psalm 18:31-34

"For who is God, except the LORD?
And who is a rock, except our God?
It is God who arms me with strength,
And makes my way perfect.
He makes my feet like the feet of deer,
And sets me on my high places.
He teaches my hands to make war,
So that my arms can bend a bow of bronze."

Who is God?

God is a _____ .

Who am I?

I am _____ .

Example:

_____

_____

_____

_____

_____

_____

_____

Psalm 18:35-36

"You have also given me the shield of Your salvation;

Your right hand has held me up,

Your gentleness has made me great.

You enlarged my path under me,

So my feet did not slip."

Who is God?

God is a _____ .

Who am I?

I am _____ .

Example:

_____

_____

_____

_____

_____

_____

_____

_____

Psalm 18:37-42

"I have pursued my enemies and overtaken them;

Neither did I turn back again till they were destroyed.

I have wounded them,

So that they could not rise;

They have fallen under my feet.

For You have armed me with strength for the battle;

You have subdued under me those who rose up against me.

You have also given me the necks of my enemies,

So that I destroyed those who hated me.

They cried out, but there was none to save;

Even to the LORD, but He did not answer them.

Then I beat them as fine as the dust before the wind;

I cast them out like dirt in the streets."

Who is God?

God is a _____ .

Who am I?

I am _____ .

Example:

_____

_____

_____

_____

_____

_____

_____

Psalm 18:43-45

"You have delivered me from the strivings of the people;

You have made me the head of the nations;

A people I have not known shall serve me.

As soon as they hear of me they obey me;

The foreigners submit to me.

The foreigners fade away,

And come frightened from their hideouts."

Who is God?

God is a _____ .

Who am I?

I am _____ .

Example:

_____

_____

_____

_____

_____

_____

Psalm 18:46-49

"The LORD lives!

Blessed be my Rock!

Let the God of my salvation be exalted.

It is God who avenges me,

And subdues the peoples under me;

He delivers me from my enemies.

You also lift me up above those who rise against me;

You have delivered me from the violent man.

Therefore I will give thanks to You, O LORD, among the Gentiles,

And sing praises to Your name."

Who is God?

God is a   .

Who am I?

I am   .

Example:

Psalm 18:50

"Great deliverance He gives to His king,

And shows mercy to His anointed,

To David and his descendants forever more."

Who is God?

God is a _____ .

Who am I?

I am _____ .

Example:

_____

_____

_____

_____

_____

_____

_____

JOURNAL

Speak forth your faith. Make a list of God's faithfulness. This should include accomplishments, what God has allowed you to experience or overcome, and what you will overcome. Examples are conquering sickness, disease, poverty, oppression, and fear. You can also make statements of faith like, "I have faith that I will walk in health, prosperity, and joy."

The Great Exchange of Jesus' Life for My Life

In this section, we will dive into the significance of our value in God in terms of God sending His Son. Understanding who God is helps us to know ourselves more.

To begin, think about this question: How well do you receive and/or believe the truth? Is your mind convinced of the truth? Are you convinced of the truth?

Proverbs 23:7 reminds us that we are who we think we are. Luke 6:45 reminds us that we act out and live out what is in our heart. The more we believe we are God's chosen children, the more we will live out the life that He has for us. Sometimes it is hard to believe a person would give his life as exchange for ours. Jesus, the Wonderful Counselor, Mighty God, Everlasting Father, and Prince of Peace, gave His life for our life so that we can reap love, joy, peace, patience, kindness, goodness, faithfulness, humility, and self-control. Read Isaiah 9:6 and Galatians 5:22-23.

Jesus exchanged His life for our lives. Our lives were not up to par; instead, they were shameful, not worthy to be saved, disgraceful and embarrassing, destitute, covered by guilt, and ruled by jealousy. Our lives should have led us to death; there should have been no love from the Creator. We should have been cast out and not forgiven. But God made the greatest exchange. Read Isaiah 53:3-5. He sent His only Son to give us His life so that we can reap the rewards of His life. This is not by what we did. We cannot and will never be able to afford to pay back what God has done for us. But we can live out what is now rightfully ours, a purposed life, a chosen life where we are protected and fearless. In the next exercise, we will examine our own outcome of that great exchange and how that great exchange has impacted our lives.

Why Is My Value Significant?

Remember Genesis 22:7-8, the conversation between Isaac and his father Abraham: "But Isaac spoke to Abraham his father and said, 'My father!' And he said, 'Here I am, my son.' Then he said, 'Look, the fire and the wood, but where is the lamb for a burnt offering?' And Abraham said, 'My son, God will provide for Himself the lamb for a burnt offering.' So the two of them went together."

It would be hard for a father to steady his voice and with confidence respond that God will supply the sacrifice needed. How did God feel when He told His Son He was going to sacrifice Him for people that may not appreciate the sacrifice? Think about Jesus as the sacrifice. Jesus knew the outcome of His obedience. In obeying God, Jesus became the sacrifice and gave His life.

What was the obedience of Jesus?

What did Jesus sacrifice?

What was the outcome?

How do we obey God in our toughest challenges?

What are the outcomes for others in our obedience?

Take away this: As we desire that our walk of life become more like Jesus' walk, we must desire to be obedient and to sacrifice. There are idiosyncrasies that we must give up to become more like Jesus. Examples include the way we think, what we allow to rest in our hearts, those whom we allow to influence us, and what we watch and hear. These are only a few. Giving these up allows for a change to happen in us.

Protected in Life by God

The suggested reading is 1 Samuel 29 – 2 Samuel 5.

Before a challenge, David sought direction from the Lord as noted in 2 Samuel 5:19. Not only did he ask if he should pursue the opportunity he had but also if it would be successful. In the end, David was successful and defeated the Philistines. David inquired of the Lord again in 2 Samuel 5:23. This time the Lord gave a different plan of action. Instead of going up, they circled around the Philistines. Same problem, different answer. God will not allow the enemy to take you. You may be challenged multiple times, but you will not lose. Read Psalm 121. God sent His only Son for us to have everlasting life abundantly. He will not let anyone or anything take what He has tremendously purchased. He purchased us with the blood of Jesus. We are jewels to God, more precious than we can think.

You may be in a situation that you have been in before. Be confident that God will again provide a way out. We deal with different situations which are actually the very same all the time. Think of missionaries who depend on God for financial resources each month. Every month is the same, but God may provide a different way of sustaining them. We may deal with health issues, broken hearts, and insecurities. When we take our concerns to God, He always provides an answer, regardless if we recently came to

Him with the same concerns. Each time, God is faithful to hear us and provide yet again an answer. Let the challenges bring you closer to God by continually giving Him your challenge so He can provide a way out.

Make three lists on the following pages:

1. *What has God anointed you to do.*

2. *What has God delivered you from.*

3. *What has God blessed you with (or given to you).*

What has God anointed you to do:

Anointed examples: serve, teach/minister to children, evangelize, exhort, counsel, witness to others, encourage, motivate, perform acts of kindness, lead, be an example, be gracious/ hospitable, worship, spread the Gospel, show thankfulness, be a connector, fight for justice, love music or art, show empathy, speak things into existence, show patience, pray, advocate for children, give, be fearless, create.

What has God delivered you from:

Delivered examples: shame, drugs, alcoholism, smoking, cursing, generational curse, grudge, fear, meaninglessness, unworthiness, anger, pride, lupus, unforgiveness, lust, porn, rejection, darkness, anxiety, doubt, debt, eternal death, unemployment, depression, unworthiness, abuse, not believing in yourself, loneliness, bad choices, bad relationships, low self-esteem, judgment, poverty, self-righteousness, depending on employer as resource, sickness.

What has God blessed you with (or given to you):

Blessed examples: new life, family, drawings, children, church, worship, dancing, peace, service, wisdom, communication, joy, good health, skill, intercessory prayer, small groups, helping others, counseling, music, abundance, self-control, courage, writing, discernment, job, protection, provision, friends, patience, compassion, laughter, appreciation of life, knowledge, shelter, understanding, talent, kindness, fruit of the Spirit.

Take away this: This exercise allows you to see how far you have come with God on your side. We often do not think how far God has brought us, especially when we are in challenges.

My Response to Challenges

The suggested reading is 2 Samuel 5-6.

When you feel you are doing everything right but nothing is working, ask God, "How can I get into Your presence?" Your desire could be the will of God, but maybe your method does not align with God's. There was a time where David had trouble getting the ark of God to him and to his city. Read 2 Samuel 6. David left the ark at a house, which blessed that home. The presence of God brought blessings to that home. If God can bless others, then surely God can bless the City of David, Jerusalem. As the ark neared Jerusalem, David began to dance in response to his thankfulness and the blessings coming his way.

When you see others being blessed, join them. Rejoice with them. Praise God with them. Worship God for all He is doing and will do for His children. Be encouraged when you have been praying for healing and others around you are being healed. This is an indication that God hears the prayers of His children. He hears you. Show your appreciation for His nature and won-der-working power while your deliverance is on the way. Do not allow the timing of your deliverance to be a reason to stop believing. Instead, allow the deliverance of others push you to believe even more greatly in God.

List the different ways we can praise, worship, and thank God.

_____

_____

_____

_____

_____

_____

_____

_____

Why is it important to have a heart of praise and worship?

_____

_____

_____

_____

_____

_____

_____

_____

Take away this: There are many ways to praise and worship God. We can dance, sing, draw, clap, and raise our hands. We can also trust God and have patience. Our praise and worship are indicators of our trust and confidence in God. The more we praise and worship God, the more it becomes pleasing to us and not an act of requirement but of love. It builds our faith and prevents us from giving in to negative emotions.

JOURNAL

List challenges. Challenges may include dating, finances, or career. Include a past experience and one not yet conquered. Pray and ask God for how to approach the situation.

Practice Trusting God

David practiced trusting God. It started small. God being with him while he was protecting sheep from the wildlife was a major foundation for David's trust in God. That trust brought peace and calmness. When David faced Goliath, he relied once again on his trust in God.

We have to be confident in who God is so we are confident in His power. It is amazing how David put his trust in God. Through practice, David increased his own value by valuing the trust he had in God. He was 100 percent assured in God's ability to win and relied 100 percent on God to make him victorious.

Every day, declare to yourself that you are loved by God and that God is the Director of your life. Tell God who He is and who you are in Him. "God, You are strong, and, therefore, I am strong. You are a Way Maker, and, therefore, I am not bound. With You I have everything I need. You are mighty, and, therefore, I am a conqueror. For me to live out my best tomorrow, I must live my best today. I can only have my best today if I know You are the best and have my best interest at Your heart."

Let's discuss David's confidence and set a pattern of our own to practice trusting God.

Confident and Victorious

The suggested reading is 2 Samuel 7-8, 10.

Did David understand the significance of his relationship with God, as it relates to his future? Yes! Read 2 Samuel 7:16. David wanted God to complete the work He said He would in him, so God's name could be magnified. This is indicated in 2 Samuel 7:25-26. In trusting God, David's skills improved, making him one of the most notable warriors in the Bible. One challenge successfully completed led to him completing many more challenges successfully.

David's success was a result of his confidence in God. This led to his confidence increasing in himself. David had an opportunity to confront Goliath with the best armor. He refused it as noted in 1 Samuel 17:38-40. In 1 Samuel 17:45-46, David specifically stated that he would cut off Goliath's head. Keep in mind that David had no armor and only stones as he made this strong statement. There is no way David could have cut off Goliath's head with only stones. David was confident that our powerful God would make him successful. As always, David was correct about God. David ultimately took hold of Goliath's head.

Here is a recap of David's accomplishments and victories. Notice his growth over time.

- Killed Goliath (1 Samuel 17:51)
- Killed 200 Philistines (1 Samuel 18:27)

- Fought the Philistines (1 Samuel 19:8)
- Raided nations (1 Samuel 27:8)
- Became king (2 Samuel 5:3)
- Killed 18,000 Syrians (2 Samuel 8:13)
- Killed 40,700 Syrians (2 Samuel 10:18)

You may not feel that you are growing, but you are growing. Completing this study shows that you care about your relationship with God and you are intently seeking to know how to please Him more. Be confident that you are growing and you are becoming stronger in the process.

Push forward by challenging yourself to be greater. How can you continue your growth in confidence?

What is the result of having confidence in our faith?

Take away this: Confidence in our faith will lead to success and defeating the enemy. We live a valued life by trusting God and being assured of who He is. Live confidently by knowing you are forgiven.

Sharpened by Setting Patterns

The suggested reading is 2 Samuel 11.

David should have been at war. He chose to not be involved in a task that was required of his position. There are times when we rest and times that we truly focus. When we should be focused, stay focused. David may have been tired or just did not want to be in battle. If he was in battle (and should have been in battle), then he would not have been able to make the choice of adultery with Bathsheba. The opportunity would not have existed. This one decision led to multiple sins, including the death of an innocent man and a child, and involved others in the plot of murder.

To avoid willfully sinning, we must be occupied with God's business. We should be serving to expand His kingdom. We should have accountability partners to inform us when something does not look right about the decisions we are making. When we become less concerned about time and the commitment we are making with our time, we can put ourselves in unnecessary situations that can lead to actions that are unfavorable to our future.

Decisions we make can cause us to value ourselves less. We committed to the actions and received the consequence. As we deal with the results of shame and guilt, we see ourselves as unfit to be a child of God. Gratefully, God sent

Jesus to give His life and take our sins so that we can be in right standing with God. God has a plan in place to bring our value back to us. It is not the sin that defines who we are. Our relationship with God defines us. Ask for forgiveness for the sin.

It can be difficult to accept that God is so loving and that He still reaches to us so that we can be next to Him. Now that we know that God is so loving, let us put a plan together to avoid willfully sinning and going through the cycle of shame and guilt again.

Establish patterns that will keep you trusting and building confidence in God's ability. To you, this will show your identity in Him. Consider schedules by day, week, and month/season.

What patterns can you establish?
Is there a schedule you can stick to?

Daily:

_____

_____

_____

_____

_____

_____

Weekly:

_____

_____

_____

_____

_____

_____

Monthly/Seasonally:

Take away this: We can set a pattern of our own by studying the Word, having accountability partners, attending Bible studies and small groups, and becoming involved in ministries. Become involved in your church. Proverb 27:17 confirms that as iron sharpens iron, so we sharpen each other's character. Being around others in faith will help you to become sharpened in God's Word.

Discovery of My Support Through Scripture

In the next pages, we will review verses that encourage us to live the life that God has given us. You will first receive two verses and discover how to use those verses to live a life of a champion. Next, there are two additional verses that you should study and think on or about. There are questions to help you dive deeply into the study of the verse so you can know for yourself how to incorporate the verses into your everyday life.

Verse Discovery

"For God has not given us a spirit of fear, but of power and of love and of a sound mind." 2 Timothy 1:7

Situations can instill fear in us. The unknown will cause us to fear what lies ahead. Studying this verse encourages us not to fear but to remember the gift of the Holy Spirit. You can dive deeply in studying this verse in four specific areas. They are understanding fear, power, love, and a sound mind.

Fear

Fear is not from God. Fear in this text is timidity and cowardice (lack of bravery, weakness). Cowardice is the opposite of strength, courage, and trust. We are reminded of the spiritual gift we already have which gives us power, love, and a sound mind.

Power

Power refers to the higher force working in a lower being, causing that being to become mighty. This is where we are strengthened and can be courageous in our life.

Love

Love in this text is love that is not an impulse or natural feeling. This love includes loving those who are unworthy. This is a deep love and is the fruit of the Spirit. In other words, the Spirit produces (or generates, causes) us to love.

Sound Mind

Sound mind is also known as self-discipline and self-control. Not controlling the situation but controlling our reaction to the situation.

So, here is where we choose: Do we live a life of fear, or do we live a life of confidence and courage? A life of fear controls the situation, not first seeking God. The life of confidence and courage allows the spirit of God to strengthen us every day, being spirit-led, not feeling-led. This life allows God to lead while we control how we respond.

I encourage you to remember the gift of the Spirit that was given to you and is in you.

Verse Discovery

"For God so loved the world, that He gave his only begotten Son, that whoever believes in Him should not perish, but have everlasting life." John 3:16

God's gift to the world is not just life but an everlasting life.

This verse records part of a conversation that is between Nicodemus (a Jewish leader) and Jesus. The foundation of this everlasting life is the love of God. It is not contingent on whether love is received back; rather, God's love is given freely to everyone, including those who are unworthy.

The word "begotten" indicates "only one." The Son did not earn the title for His works. He did not become His Son. He was His Son from the beginning of time. "To Perish" can be defined as being destroyed, lost, or dying. You do not need to be dead to have everlasting life; you can have it now if you believe.

In this verse we are given two options: to believe or not to believe. Believing gives us eternal life. Not believing leads to condemnation. However, the inspiration is not to condemn but to have us believe. The conversation between Nicodemus and Jesus is very specific. This conversation revealed many things, one of them regarding the love of God. I suggest spending time meditating on how this love seeks and desires us to have the life that God wants us to have and the life that God will maintain for us.

Verse Study

"And the second is like it: 'You shall love your neighbor as yourself.'"
Matthew 22:39

How does self-love play a role in this verse?

Who are "neighbors"?

Is it truly possible to love neighbors fully without first loving yourself?

What are ways to love your neighbor?

Why is this the second commandment?

How does this verse strengthen us?

What other verses can support this verse?

Verse Study

"But the fruit of the Spirit is love, joy, peace, longsuffering, kindness, goodness, faithfulness, gentleness, self-control. Against such there is no law."
Galatians 5:22-23

Explore each characteristic: love, joy, peace, longsuffering, kindness, goodness, faithfulness, gentleness, self-control.

List another word for each characteristic.

How does each characteristic influence our lives daily?

What is the effect on us for not having each characteristic?

What is the consequence that others feel if we do not have the entire fruit of the Spirit?

What is self-control?

How does this verse strengthen you?

JOURNAL

In John 3:16, we see that God sent His Son for us. How do you show appreciation for this gift of love?

What Is My Value?

In Section One, "What Is Value?", we discussed the term "value" and why we struggle with identity.

We discussed who God is, and, therefore, who we are in "I Am a Child of God."

In "The Great Exchange of Jesus' Life for My Life," we discussed the impact of being a child of God and the blessing that comes with it.

We discussed what confidence in God looks like and created a pattern to building our trust and confidence in God in "Practice Trusting God."

In this last section, "What Is My Value?", let us compare David again to Saul. But this time, we will add the values that he used to help him in his life. Then we will read how David became successful by first relying on God.

Values Needed to Lead Others

The suggested reading is 2 Samuel 20-21.

The story of David started with him as a shepherd. David became Saul's musician, managed different groups of people, and led nations. David went from fighting lions and bears and protecting lambs, to fighting armies and protecting God's people. David led a profitable nation. David inquired of God regarding the famine, and God responded.

We see a full circle where, in the beginning, David defeats Goliath alone to David inspiring others to defeat giants in his later years. In 2 Samuel 21, we read of four under his command having no hesitation in fighting giants: Abishai, Sibbechai, Elhanan, and Jonathan (son of Shimea who was David's brother). Referring to David, Saul asked in 1 Samuel 17:55-56 who he was. By the end of David's story, we understand David's purpose and his value. Who was David? David was a child of God. David was not just the son of Jesse but a true soldier in the army of the Lord.

Despite your challenges in life, your story is not over. You could be in the beginning of your walk with God, and you don't see how this will come together. Allow this story of David to encourage you. The more David looked to God for his value and strength, the more David accomplished. Today, you may be struggling through this season. Be assured God is on your side. Allow God to show you your significance in this season. Once this season is over, it will be added to your list of accomplishments of how God brought you through.

Read 1 Samuel 17 again.

Compare David's physical location in battle (2 Samuel 21:15) to Saul's (1 Samuel 17:2).

LOCATION IN BATTLE		
David	Saul	Value Needed

Compare David's servants (2 Samuel 21:15-22) to Saul's (1 Samuel 17:11, 24).

SERVANTS		
David	Saul	Value Needed

Compare David's leadership in battle with the Philistines (2 Samuel 21:15) to Saul's (1 Samuel 17:25).

LEADERSHIP		
David	Saul	Value Needed

Can you now see David's objective in battles?
Reference 1 Samuel 17:26 and 34-36.

At the end of David's journey, can you see why
God chose him?
Note your takeaway.

God Is the Source of My Value

The suggested reading is 2 Samuel 22.

Think of the issues David had and how God delivered him from the issues. David intently refers to God as his source for help and acknowledges his dependency on Him in 2 Samuel 22:2. God was his source of refuge in times of trouble in verse three. God was salvation to David when Saul hunted to kill him in verse four. Verse seven shows that whenever David had a problem, he called on the Lord who heard him. In this chapter, we see David not only gives credit to God for his success, but he also includes why. 2 Samuel 22:31-51 details how he was victorious, which was by God. David's value was not in his status, appearance, skill, or ability, but in his identity in God. The Lord gave him strength, speed, and stability to overwhelm the enemy.

In the same way, God makes us successful if we look to him. David's journey with God was a commitment. Every day he had to rely on God to reinforce him. Every day David had to know that God was his true and only source for victory. This was a constant effort. It is easy to be distracted by the economic issues, political conversations, and cultural struggles. These can all take our eyes off of God and have us move toward what society values. You must remain committed to God so that He can show you who you are and how you can live successfully through Him.

Your value to God is more significant than you could ever think. One definition for "value" is "the worth of something in terms of the amount of other things for which it can be exchanged" (Dictionary.com). God exchanged His Son for your life so you could live a life in abundant joy, peace, and hope.

How do you define your value?

_____

_____

_____

Describe challenges in your life and the value attributes you will use to overcome the challenges.

Challenge	Value Needed

JOURNAL

Read each part of 2 Samuel 22. Place statements of value next to each verse (examples: "protected," "confident," "loved," "worthy").